Origami Boxes

FOR GIFTS, TREASURES & TRIFLES

Origami Boxes
FOR GIFTS, TREASURES & TRIFLES

Alexandra Dirk

Sterling Publishing Co., Inc.
New York

Photos by Thomas Weiss
Illustrated by Gisela Thommel
Translated by Annette Englander

Library of Congress Cataloging-in-Publication Data

Dirk, Alexandra.
[Origami-Schachteln English]
Origami boxes : for gifts, treasures & trifles / Alexandra Dirk.
   p.   cm.
Includes index.
ISBN 0-8069-9495-9
1. Box making. 2. Origami. 3. Ornamental boxes. I. Title.
TT870.5.D5613   1997
736′.982—dc21   96-46685
                                            CIP

10 9 8 7 6 5 4 3 2 1

Published 1995 by Sterling Publishing Company, Inc.
387 Park Avenue South, New York, N.Y. 10016
Previously published in Germany by Ravensburger Buchverlag
under the title *Origami Schachteln*
© 1995 by Ravensburger Buchverlag
New edition of © 1993 version of hobby courses *Origami Schachteln*
Translation © 1997 by Sterling Publishing Company, Inc.
Distributed in Canada by Sterling Publishing
% Canadian Manda Group, One Atlantic Avenue, Suite 105
Toronto, Ontario, Canada M6K 3E7
Distributed in Great Britain and Europe by Cassell PLC
Wellington House, 125 Strand, London WC2R 0BB, England
Distributed in Australia by Capricorn Link (Australia) Pty Ltd.
P.O. Box 6651, Baulkham Hills, Business Centre, NSW 2153, Australia
Manufactured in the United States of America

Sterling ISBN 0-8069-9495-9

Table of Contents

Introduction

With this book, you can create beautiful folding boxes for wrapping small gifts and little presents as well as for storing jewelry, buttons, coins, and keepsakes.

The techniques presented here are best called "combination Origami" because of their "practical" variation on the traditional art of paper folding. In contrast to the classical Origami technique, where all figures are created out of only one sheet of paper, the boxes here are made (depending on their form) out of three, four, six, or even eight sheets. These same-sized papers are folded individually and then connected with each other by putting them together. This book will concentrate on square boxes whose bottom and lid consist of four sheets each.

They are best suited for learning the "combination Origami" easily and with fast success.

The Origami master Tomoko Fuse, who is well known in Japan and considered the most important female artist of the modern "Modular Origami," developed and perfected this technique. It is based on partial elements that are folded equally and, through putting them together, form complex geometrical forms like cubes and polyhedrons as well as pretty boxes.

I encountered this kind of paper folding technique during a trip to Japan. It so fascinated me

that I learned it immediately there and, to this day, my enthusiasm for it has not lessened. I hope to share it with you in this book.

Alexandra Dirk

Material and Technique

The most fascinating aspect of Origami is that you really do not need anything else but paper. Helping devices like a pair of scissors or glue are unnecessary for our boxes because the individually folded elements are solidly combined by only slipping them into each other with some holding folds.

Choosing the right paper is more important. The effect of the folded boxes is not just determined by the folding technique but also by the kind of paper—its quality, color, and pattern—you use.

Paper

Almost any kind of paper is suitable as long as it does not tear easily or have trouble being folded. The strength of the paper influences the sturdiness and, thus, the usability of the box. If the paper is too thin, you can work with a double sheet or line the original sheet with a thin one in order to make it more durable. As a general rule, you should choose a stronger paper for the bottom than for the lid.

Besides the different precut Origami papers that are available in paper stores, you can work with every kind of gift wrapping or old paper. By using old sheet music, maps, pages from old telephone books, paper pattern charts, or newspapers, you can achieve many ingenious effects. The traditional Origami papers are generally white on the underside, but today they are also available with colors on both sides. Some boxes come out better when they are made with two-colored paper because their folded pattern produces a beautiful design. It is important to think about choosing the right paper for each project because not every box looks equally nice with every paper.

The boxes in this book can be made only with square pieces of paper. You can choose different sizes, for example 4 × 4, 5 × 5, 6 × 6, 7 × 7, 8 × 8 inches, etc. In the beginning, it is best to use the 6 × 6 in. size. If you cut your own paper, you need to be extremely accurate, which is not so simple with a pair of scissors. Use a cutting board, if possible.

Folding Technique

You need a firm, level surface when folding. It is essential that you work cleanly and accurately. Otherwise, each inaccuracy will be multiplied by the number of sheets, the individual pieces will then not fit into each other, and the box will not be sturdy.

Repeat each folding step immediately for all four sheets. Before you put the pieces together, you should always check that all the individual pieces look the same. Using paper clips can help you join them more easily. Be especially careful when you join the last piece with the first piece.

Practice the simpler models at the beginning of the book before trying the more advanced projects.

Folding Instructions

Occasionally the terms "mountain fold" and "valley fold" are used in the instructions. A mountain fold folds outward like an upside down "V." A valley fold folds inward like a regular "V."

Below is a key for following the illustrations that are shown in the individual folding steps:

- - - - - = line is being folded
——— = line is already folded
White surface = underside of paper

Dark surface = upperside of paper

This will help you orient your paper through each step of the instructions.

Bottoms

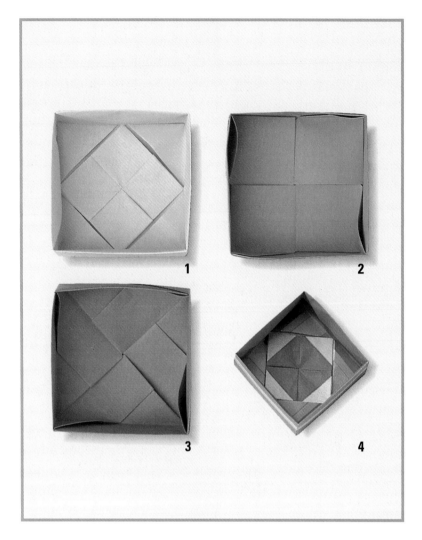

For all the boxes, the bottom must be somewhat smaller than the lid. Nevertheless, the papers used for the bottom and lid are equal in size. The smaller measurements for the bottom are made through the folding steps.

The three kinds of bottoms (pictured above) show a different pattern on the inside. Each of these bottoms can be combined with any of the twelve lid variations in this book.

Bottom 1 can be made out of papers weighing 70 to 100 g/m^2. There are two ways of fitting the individual pieces together, which again can be combined with each other. Through this, the different patterns on the inside of the bottom come about, such as in Bottom 4.

Bottom 2 should also be made out of not too-thin paper, since the individual pieces hold onto each other only slightly. This bottom has an interesting weaving pattern created on the inside.

Bottom 3 is a variation of Bottom 2 where the tips are folded over on the inside in order to ensure a better stability.

Folding Bottom 1

Work four times.

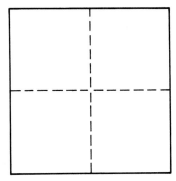

1. Fold the center horizontally and vertically, then open up these folds again.

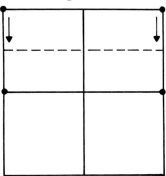

2. Fold so that the dots meet and open up again.

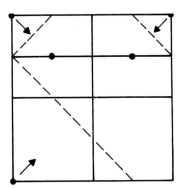

3. Make three folds by meeting the dots.

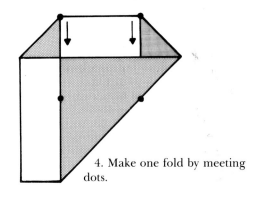

4. Make one fold by meeting dots.

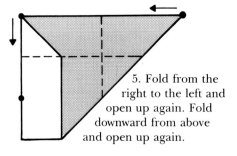

5. Fold from the right to the left and open up again. Fold downward from above and open up again.

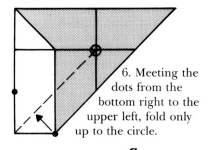

6. Meeting the dots from the bottom right to the upper left, fold only up to the circle.

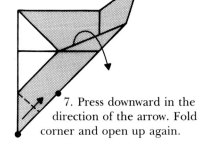

7. Press downward in the direction of the arrow. Fold corner and open up again.

Putting Together Bottom 1

First possibility: Push the right piece into the left piece. Repeat this three times until all four pieces are fitted into each other.

Second possibility: Push the left piece into the right piece. Repeat this three times.

Third possibility: Proceed first according to Picture 1, then according to Picture 2. Repeat both steps once more.

For all three possibilities, the four tips are lying on the inside at the end. To make the box sturdy, fold these tips downward at the prefolded line, as seen in the picture.

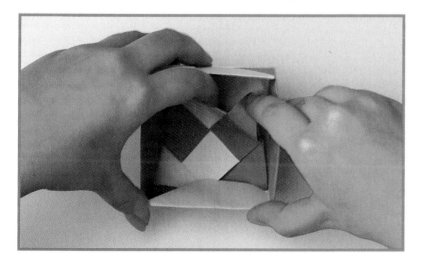

Folding Bottom 2

Work four times.

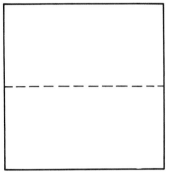

1. Fold downward along the center.

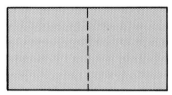

2. Fold along the center from the left to the right.

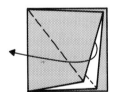

3. Open the upper layer and fold to form a triangle.

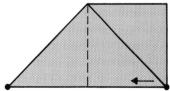

4. Fold only the right half of the triangle to the left.

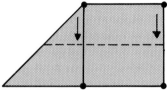

5. Meeting the dots from above downward, fold and open up again.

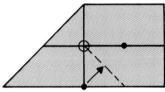

6. Meeting the dots from below upward, fold up to the circle.

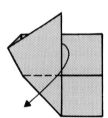

7. Press downward in direction of the arrow.

Putting Together Bottom 2

There is only one method of putting this bottom together. It must always be pushed from the right to the left, as seen in the picture. Push the upper tip of the right piece into the left piece.

Make sure that the lower tips are lying below the piece on the underside of the bottom. Repeat three times until all four pieces are fitted into each other.

To make the bottom sturdy, the tips, which are lying on the underside of the bottom, must be folded inward at the slant.

Folding Bottom 3

Work four times.
First do page 14 through step 5.

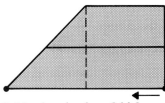 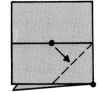

6. Meeting the dots, fold from the right to the left.

7. Meeting the dots, fold downward from above.

This is what an individual piece of Bottom 3 looks like when all the folding steps are completed

Putting Together Bottom 3

There is also only one way of putting this bottom together. Always push from the right to the left. The upper tip of the right individual piece must remain lying on top.

The lower tip of the right individual piece is pushed, from the right to the left, into the left individual piece. Repeat three times until all parts are stuck into each other.

To make the bottom sturdy, the tips that are lying on the inside are folded under at the slant.

Lid Variations

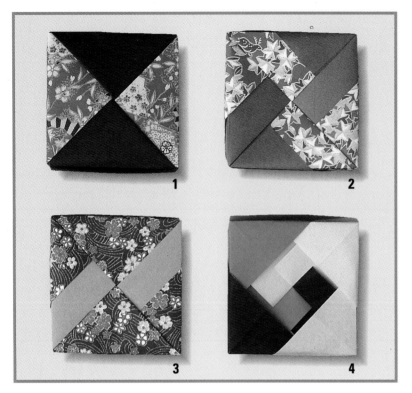

1

2

3

4

It is really amazing that, with a few different folding steps and assembling possibilities, twelve completely different looking lids are created for always the same square box. In addition, there are the many more possible variations that can be obtained solely from the choice of paper.

The first three kinds of lid are made from the same folding steps. The different patterns are created, just like Bottom 1, solely through the different ways of putting them together.

Lid 1 should be folded out of two or four different papers.

Lids 2 and 3 come out the best when you mix colored paper with patterned paper.

Since the patterns for Bottom 1 and Lids 1 to 3 are identical, you should use them to make boxes. Working with complementary paper and the same method of putting them together will give you an especially balanced combination.

Lid 4 is a folding variation of Lids 1 to 3. It can only be put together in one way. More patterns can be created from the completed lid with the corners lying on top. Bottoms 1 to 3 can be used with this lid.

Lid Variations

Folding Lids 1 to 3

Work four times.

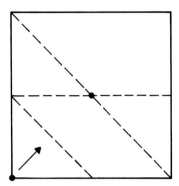

1. Fold the center horizontally and open up this fold again. Then make a fold by meeting the dots.

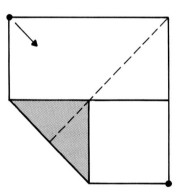

2. Make this fold by meeting the dots.

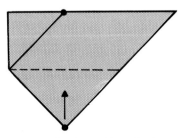

3. Meet the dots with only the top piece of the bottom corner. Fold upward and open up.

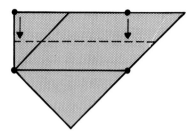

4. Fold downward and open up.

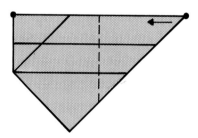

5. Fold from the right to the left and open up.

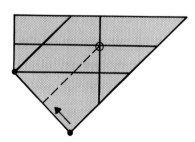

6. Meet both corners and fold upward until the circle. Keep it folded.

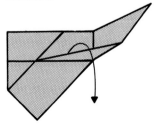

7. Press downward in the direction of the arrow.

Putting Together Lid 1

Hold the edge of the lid upward and push the right piece over the left one. Repeat three times until all four pieces are combined.

At the inside of the completed lid, you see four corners lying open. This lid is sturdy, so you don't need to make any more folds.

The outside of the completed lid has four equal-sized triangles. Experimenting with papers of different colors and patterns can produce interesting results.

Lid Variations

Putting Together Lid 2

With this lid, the right individual piece is pushed into the left one. Repeat this three times until all four pieces are fitted into each other.

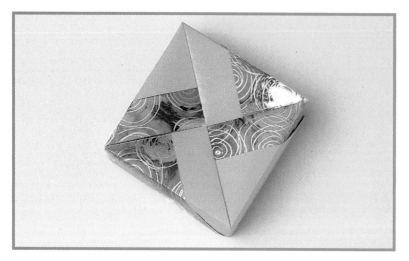

This is what the completed lid looks like. The four corners stand out from the contrasting papers. The inside pattern of this lid is the same as in Lid 1.

Putting Together Lid 3

This lid mixes the methods of putting together Lids 1 and 2. First push the right piece into the left piece.

Turn both pieces to the left and push the third piece from the right over the second piece. Insert the fourth piece like the second piece.

The pattern of the completed lid (top box in the picture) shows two stripes, which disappear in the edge of the lid. You can also mix up the methods of putting together Lids 1, 2, and 3. The lid at the bottom of the picture was created that way.

Folding Lid 4

Work four times.
First do page 20 through step 2.

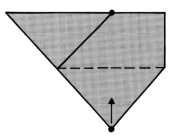

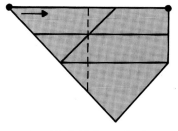

3. Meet the dots with only the top piece of the bottom corner. Fold upward and open up this fold again.

5. Make this fold from the left to the right.

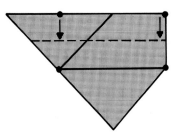

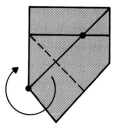

4. Fold downward and open up.

6. Meet the dots by folding upward and to the back.

This is what a completely folded individual piece of Lid 4 looks like.

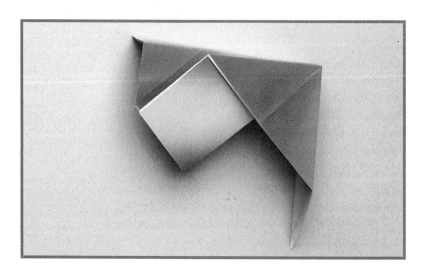

Putting Together Lid 4

Hold the pieces with the edge of the lid facing down. The right piece is pushed into the left one. Repeat three times until all four pieces are combined.

This is what the completed lid looks like from the outside. The four corners, which lie on the inside of Lids 1 to 3, are now visible on the outside. More patterns can be created by changing these corners.

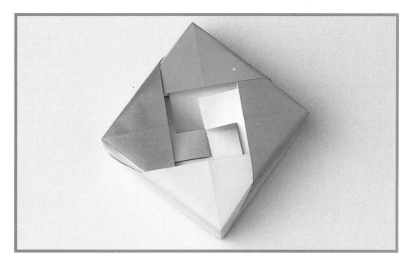

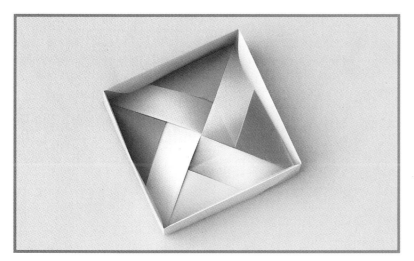

From the inside, Lid 4 resembles the outside of Lid 2.

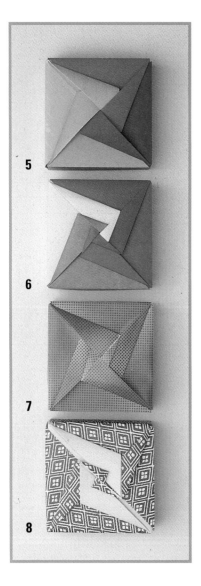

5

6

7

8

Lids 5 to 8 require a little more skill. But once you have made the first four lids several times you would have had some practice before trying your hand at these somewhat more difficult models.

As you will see in the illustrations, the patterns have a lot more three-dimensional effect than the first four lids. In Lids 5 to 8, you can create patterns on the outside and inside of the lids that are independent of one another. This happens after they have been put together. The outer and inner corners are then worked on again. This additional work on the tips must be done carefully. The three-dimensional effect is best achieved with papers weighing between 60 and 80 g/m². These not-too-strong papers best handle the somewhat tricky folding and shaping steps. Lids 5 and 6 can be made out of one, two, or four different papers. On the other hand, Lids 7 and 8 should be made out of only two different papers because otherwise the folding pattern does not come out as well.

Lid Variations

Folding Lids 5 to 8

Work four times.

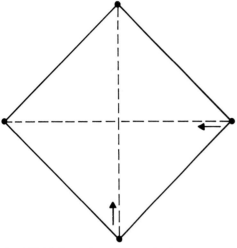

1. a) Fold from the right to the left and open up the fold. b) Make fold upward and leave it folded.

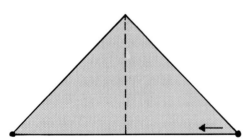

2. Fold from the right to the left and open up again.

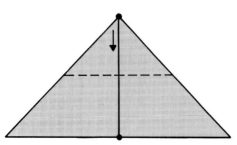

3. Fold only the top piece of the corner downward and open up again.

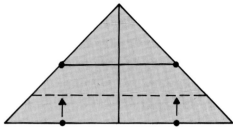

4. Meeting the dots, fold and open up again. Then open the sheet completely to reveal the underside.

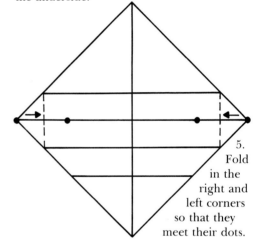

5. Fold in the right and left corners so that they meet their dots.

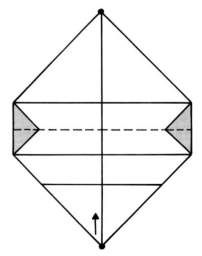

6. Fold back together by meeting the dots.

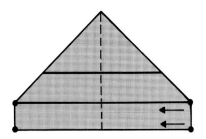 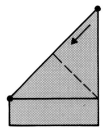

7. Fold from the right to the left.

8. Meet the dots by folding downward.

9. Fold only the piece that was folded downward in step 8 upward to meet the dots.

After folding, take the completed piece in your hands as shown in the picture. With the upper sheet, make the valley fold into a mountain fold and place it upward, to the right, on the edge. Place the lower sheet to the left (as shown in the picture on the far right).

Now fold both tips back towards the center.

Putting Together Lid 5

Hold the edge of the lid downward and push the right piece over the left piece. Repeat three times until all four pieces are fitted into each other. The tips, lying on the top and bottom, remain free.

Before you continue to work, check that four tips are lying both on the outside and inside of the lid. Now tuck the tips of the outside lid clockwise one under the other. Push the last tip under the first one.

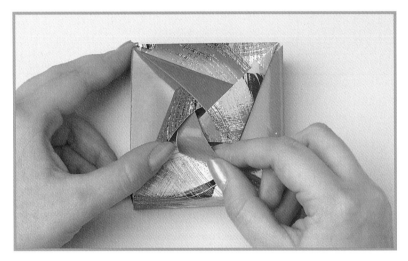

Do the same thing with tips lying on the inside. If the folded tips have too much tension, simply make them a little bit flatter.

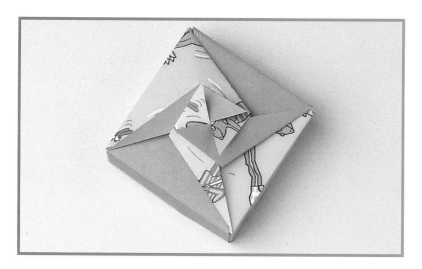

Putting Together Lid 6

Push all four individual pieces together as in Lid 5. Then place the tips that are lying on the outside one below the other in a clockwise manner so that a square made of four triangles is formed.

Now fold these triangles individually back clockwise, as seen in the picture, onto the middle diagonal; the second tip over the first one, etc. While doing this, use your other hand to support the piece from underneath.

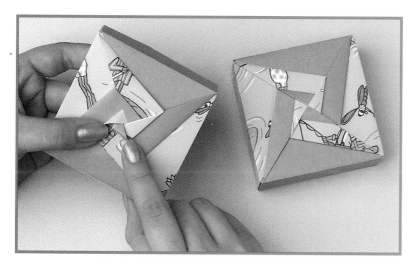

The last tip is again placed under the first one. Then proceed with the tips on the inside just as described for Lid 5.

Putting Together Lid 7

As in Lid 5, push the right piece over the left piece. Repeat three times until all individual pieces have been fitted together. Place two of the tips, which are lying opposite each other on the outside, downward. Place the other two on top. Now continue to work on the two upper tips as described for Lid 6.

To make the lid sturdy, now push these two new little tips below one another, as seen in the picture. The tips on the inside of the lid can be further worked on as you like.

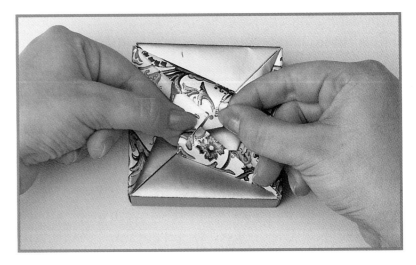

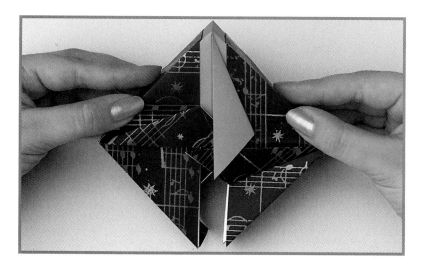

Putting Together Lid 8

When putting the four pieces together, you should alternate so that only one color becomes visible around the edge of the lid. Therefore, push the second piece from the right into the first piece. Insert the third one from the right over the second one. The fourth.one is fitted like the second one.

The four tips on the outside of the lid are placed like Lid 6. But this time, fold only two opposite tips onto the vertical diagonal. Then fold the bent tips again towards the horizontal diagonal.

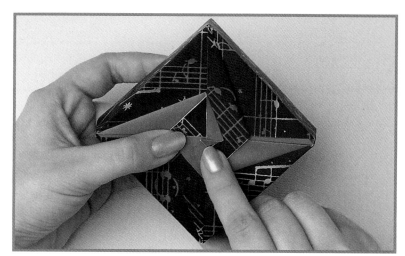

Push the tips, which are now very tiny, below one another as described for Lid 7. With some patience, this produces an especially beautiful motif. For the inside of the lid, you can follow the method for lids 5, 6, or 7.

Lid Variations

Work four times.
First do page 28 through step 6.

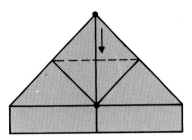

7. Meet the dots with only the top piece of the corner. Fold downward and leave it folded.

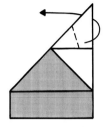

9. Fold only the inside backwards as in step 9 on page 29.

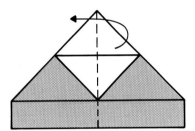

8. Fold together in half.

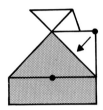

10. Meeting the dots, make the fold.

Lid 9 (picture on the right). Totally different effects can be made using this pattern. The motif, which resembles a bow or a windmill, is especially decorative. By using different colors, the effect can be even further enhanced. You should always work with two-colored paper: the upperside and underside of the paper should have a different color or pattern.

Before you make your box, you should determine what color the edge of the lid should be and what color you want to have on the corners, which are lying on the outside.

This is what a completely folded individual piece of Lid 9 looks like. Using two-colored paper clearly brings out the design.

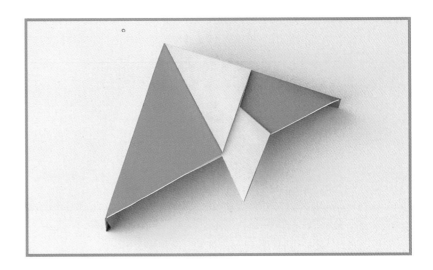

Putting Together Lid 9

The edge of the lid is again held downward. To make the lid sturdy, always push the right piece over the left one. Repeat this three times until all four pieces are connected.

Before you continue, make sure your box looks like this. To make the small triangles, place the tips below one another, as in Lid 6.

As in Lid 6, place these triangles crosswise onto the diagonal. While doing this, please use your other hand to support the piece from underneath.

The last tip is again pushed under the first one. To make sure that the lid is sturdy enough, the four little tips should meet in the middle.

The completed lid from the outside and the inside. Because of the additional large triangles on the outside, no pattern is created on the inside.

Lid Variations

Lid 10

You should always work with two-colored paper when you make this lid. The color of the underside (in the picture: white) then appears as a star on the lid. Before you begin to work, you should therefore decide how you want to design your lid using the two colors of the paper. There is no pattern created on the inside.

Lid 11

You should also work with two-colored paper for this version. Before you begin to work, you must also determine the color of the upperside and the underside of the paper. The lid in the picture on the left used red as the underside in order to bring out the "star" design. There is no pattern on the inside of this lid.

Lid 12

Of the three lid variations on this page, Lid 12 is the most elaborate one. It also has no pattern on the inside. All three lids are folded very similarly. By combining the way they are put together with the different-colored papers, more designs can be created, as shown on page 39.

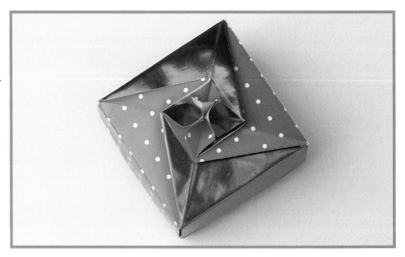

Putting Together Lid 10

You can either fit the four pieces together by following the method for Lid 5 or Lid 8. Since there is no pattern created on the inside of the lid, you will have two tips lying on top of each other on the outside. Work on the upper tips as you did for Lid 6.

Folding Lid 10

Work four times.
First do pages 28–29 through step 7.

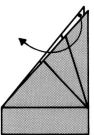

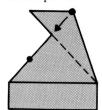

8. Fold only the inner piece of tip forward.

9. Meet the dots from the right to the left by folding in front of the piece.

10. Meet the dots now by folding downward.

Folding Lid 11

Work four times.
First do pages 28–29 through step 7 and page 40 through step 8.

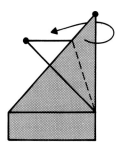
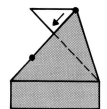

9. Meet the dots from the right to the left by folding behind the piece.

10. Meet the dots now by folding downward.

Putting Together Lid 11

You can also put the pieces together as you did for Lid 5. More patterns can be made by using different-colored papers. Also, individual colors can be made to especially stand out by using the different ways of putting the four pieces together, as in Lid 8. After you have put the pieces together, work on the upper tips as you did for Lid 6.

Folding Lid 12

Work four times.
First do pages 28–29
through step 7 and page
40 through step 10.

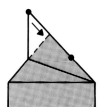

11. Fold only the top
piece of the tip from the
left to the right, meeting
the dots. Then open this
little tip like a flower.

Putting Together Lid 12

In the picture on the left, the red
underside of the blue individual
piece lies at the upper tip on the
outside. The yellow underside lies
in the tip of the green individual
piece. In order to achieve this,
the tip, lying on the inside, must
be turned over at step 8.

Lid 12 can be put together in the
same way as for Lids 10 and 11.
The opened tips for the individual pieces should be flattened be-
forehand so that the paper does
not tear. Open them up again at
the end.

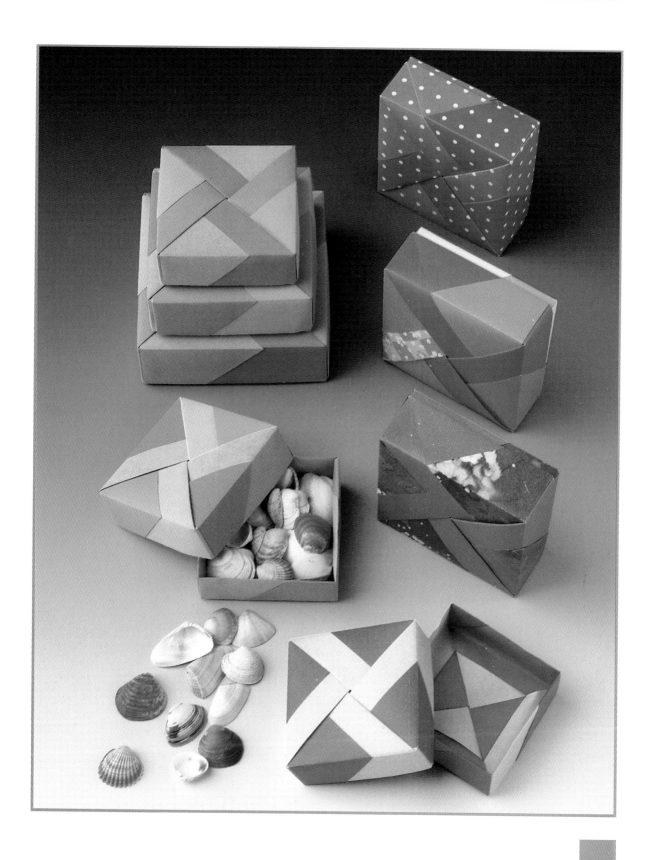

Flat Square Boxes

What makes the boxes shown on page 43 special is that the bottom and the lid for each box are the same height. Therefore, when the box is closed, the edge of the bottom is covered by the edge of the lid.

Because of their matching height, the lid and bottom are therefore folded in the same way. For the bottom, there is, per individual piece, merely one additional fold necessary so that the completed bottom is somewhat smaller than the lid.

You should always work with two-colored paper so that the beauty of the pattern is more prominent. The outside and inside can have an additional pattern if you use two papers of different colors rather than four papers of the same kind. The examples shown on page 43 are some of the possibilities that can be made.

Before you begin to work, you should determine what color you want as your upper side and underside.

Folding Flat Square Box
(Bottom and Lid)

Work four times.

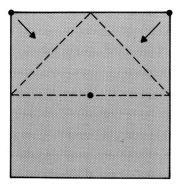

1. Fold the center. Then meet the dots by folding the two upper corners towards the center.

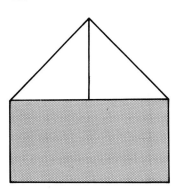

2. Turn the piece over to the underside.

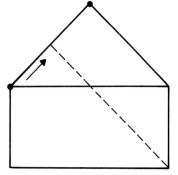

3. Meet the dots by folding the left corner upward. Open up this fold again.

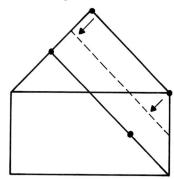

4. Fold only the top piece downward. Meet the dots and leave it folded.

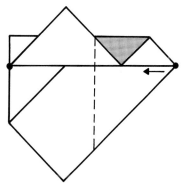

5. Fold from the right to the left.

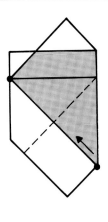

6. Meet the dots by folding upward. Open up the fold again to look like step 5.

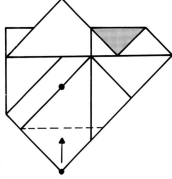

7. Fold the lower tip upward. Leave it folded.

Forming

To form the individual piece, turn it 90° counterclockwise from its position in step 7. Bring the right edge to the left so that it meets the vertical center-line. Leave it folded as shown in the far left picture. Then fold the vertical-standing tip downward to the right so that an angle is created (see picture on the left).

Now place the smaller tip that is still standing upright also downward. The picture on the far right shows the completely formed individual piece.

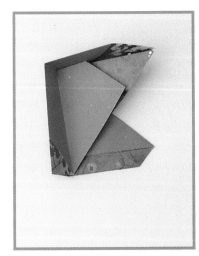

Bottom

For the bottom, an additional fold is made on the right after step 7. Use the folded triangle at the vertical center-line as a reference point for the height of the fold. Follow according to the picture.

Putting Together

Always push the right piece over the left piece. Hold the edges upward and make sure that the tip in the center of the box slides from the left into the right piece. Repeat three times until all four pieces are stuck together.

When fitting the pieces together, you must be careful, since the size difference between bottom and lid is only very slight. Any inaccuracies have an immediate effect on the fitting of the bottom and lid. The bottom and lid have the same pattern on the inside and outside.

High Square Box

All the square boxes shown so far have always the same, basic square form—despite their different looks from the various folding techniques, the ways of putting them together, and the choice of the paper.

Even though the high square box is also "only" quadrangular and square, it, nevertheless, has its own special form. The bottom becomes wider towards the top. The lid, whose sides taper off, is not, as in the other boxes, put over the bottom but simply placed onto it. This special form makes the high square box elegant and very decorative.

There is a higher degree of difficulty in making this box than the earlier ones shown. Therefore, you should not start with this project. Practice the simpler models first until you have achieved a certain routine.

The individual steps are presented in great detail so that you have success in making this box. Bottom and lid again are created

High Square Box

according to two different folding techniques. Due to the larger height of the bottom, you should use only papers with a weight of 90 g/m^2 or more. For the lid, a paper weighing 70 to 80 g/m^2 is sufficient. You can achieve special effects by using several papers of different color and quality for the lid, such as combining shiny paper with mat paper, or patterned paper with one-colored paper.

Folding High Square Box (Bottom)

Work four times.

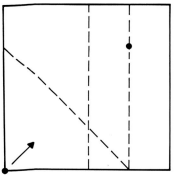

1. Fold vertically the center, then a quarter. Open these folds. Then fold upward from corner. Leave folded.

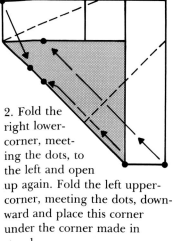

2. Fold the right lower-corner, meet-ing the dots, to the left and open up again. Fold the left upper-corner, meeting the dots, down-ward and place this corner under the corner made in step 1.

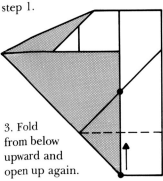

3. Fold from below upward and open up again.

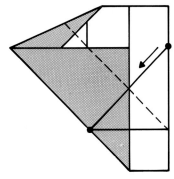

4. Fold from above downward and open up again.

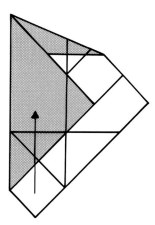

5. Bring this already folded piece upward and leave it there.

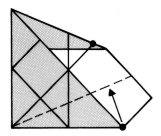

6. Meet the dots and leave it folded.

High Square Box

Forming the Bottom

After step 6, some forming needs to be done for each individual piece.

First bring the upper tip downward.

Fold the middle part, which is lying on top, downward, then upward at the already pre-folded line.

Now turn the piece over, as seen in the picture, so that you can then work on its backside.

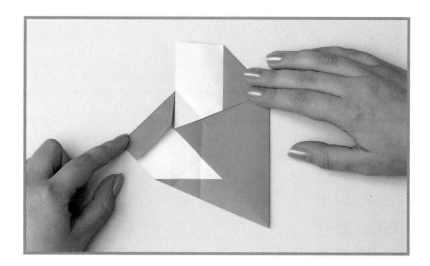

This is the backside of the piece. Fold an edge downward at the left side. In the picture, the left hand is holding down the edge.

To make the bottom sturdier, some of the already folded lines must be folded again. First rotate the piece 90° counterclockwise. Then refold the lines from below upward, as shown in the picture.

Then fold from the left to the right. Press down on the folds.

In order to make the forming procedures as clear as possible, we used, up to now, two-colored paper (upper side orange, underside white). On the next page, we continue with the red-colored paper from the completed model on page 48.

Open up the last two folds made from the folding procedures. It should look like the picture on the right.

Now take the piece in your hand as shown in the picture, with the edges facing downward. Place the two spots, which are marked in black, on top of each other and fold.

Here, the lines, which have been brought together, are recognizable. This last procedure is important for a good standing-surface of the bottom.

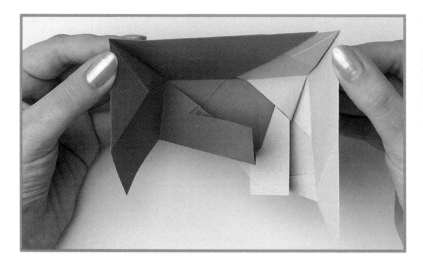

Putting Together the Bottom

Hold the edge of the bottom upward. The left piece is pushed over the right one. Repeat three times until all four pieces are connected.

Make sure that the left piece (in the picture: red) comes to lie underneath the small corner that is extending out on the outside of the right individual piece (in the picture: gray).

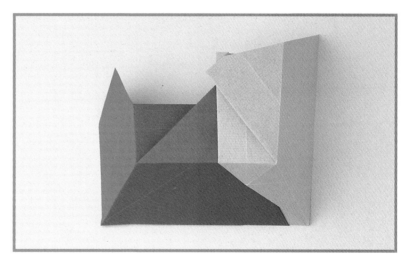

This is what the completed bottom looks like from the inside and outside. When you use four colors, the inner pattern becomes even more interesting.

55

Folding High Square Box (Lid)

Work four times.

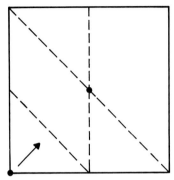

1. First fold a vertical line in the center, then a diagonal line, and open up again. Then meet the dots and open up once more.

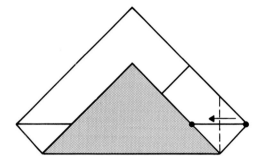

3. Fold in the right corner.

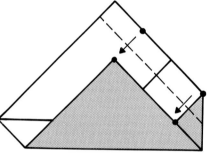

4. Fold by meeting the dots and open up again.

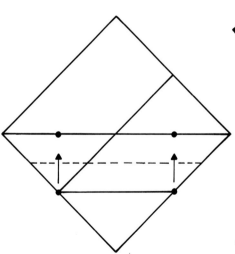

2. Make this fold by meeting the dots.

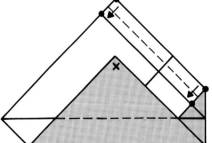

5. Make this fold and leave it folded. Fold the horizontal diagonal once more and open it up. Pull the tip, which is marked with a cross, downward and turn the piece over.

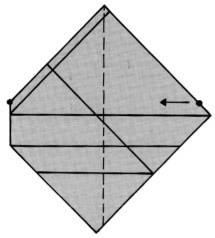

6. Meet the dots by folding from the right to the left. Leave it folded.

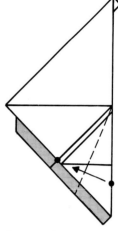

8. Meet the dots by folding from the right to the left. Open it up again. Turn the piece 180° to the left, open, and turn over to the underside.

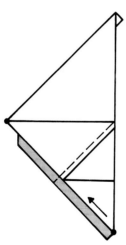

7. Meet the dots by folding from below upward. Open this fold up.

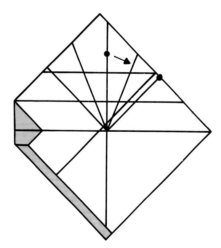

9. Meet the left dot with the right dot and leave it folded.

Forming the Lid

After step 9, the individual piece should look like this. The slant for the edge of the lid will now be made.

To do so, place the center horizontal line downward. You must make sure that the folded (now covered) angle lies only in one direction.

As shown in the picture, the upper horizontal line is now pulled apart until it lies on the lower horizontal line. Both pieces should lie smoothly on top of each other.

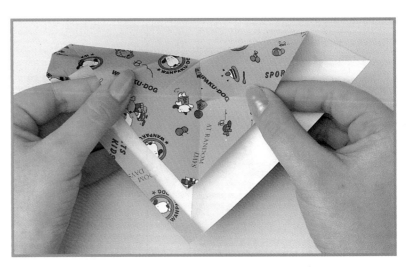

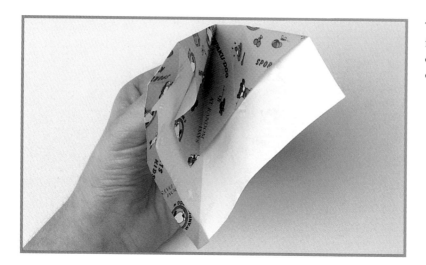

Then, the individual piece is folded together along the vertical center-line. Trace the outer lines once again.

This is what the folded-together piece should look like before you continue with the next folding steps.

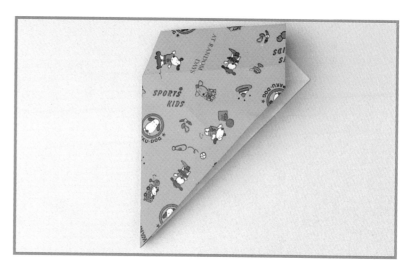

Folding Instructions after the Forming Procedures

Lid of High Square Box

1. Meet the dots by folding from below upward. Leave it folded.

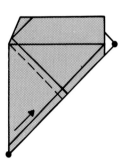

2. Fold the piece that was just folded upward back down onto the lower line. Meeting the dots, fold and leave it folded.

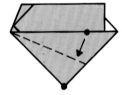

3. Fold up and open up again.

4. Meet the dots by folding from above downward. Leave it folded. Now repeat step 3 again.

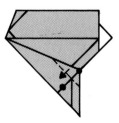

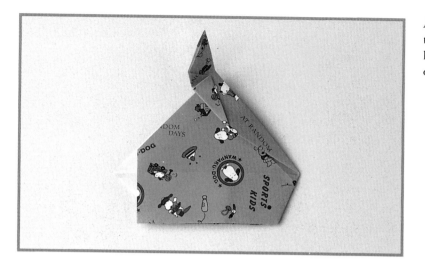

After the last four folding steps, the individual piece must look like this. Now it only needs to be opened up from the middle.

After opening it up, fold the edges of the individual piece to give it its form. In the picture at the right, you see the completed individual piece from the inside and outside.

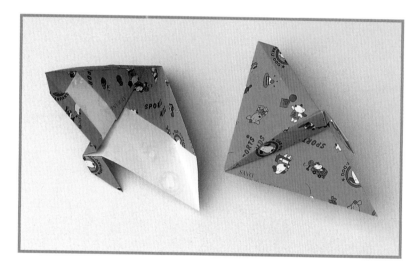

High Square Box

Putting Together the Lid

The edge of the lid must be held upward. The right piece (in the picture: red) is always pushed over the left individual piece (in the picture: green).

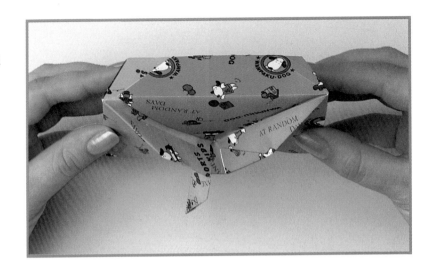

At the same time, the tip of the right (red) piece must be pushed under so that it fits into the elevation of the left (green) piece. This is clearly visible from the inside, as shown in the picture.

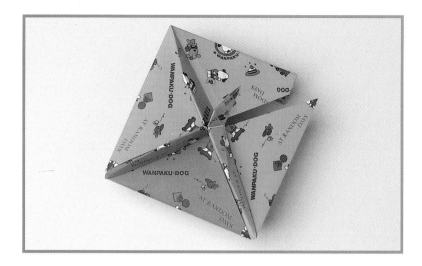

The third individual piece is pushed over the second one, the fourth over the third. You can use a pair of tweezers to help you fit the tips in the center.

This is what the completed lid looks like from the outside. The cross section forms a handle for you to comfortably lift the lid.

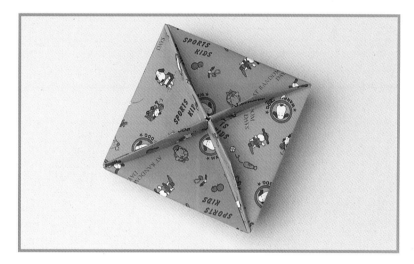

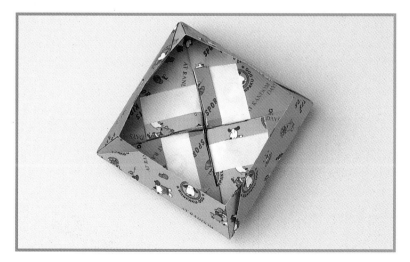

The completed lid from the in-side. If the little tips are not tucked in correctly, they can be adjusted with a pair of tweezers.

Index